Poetry

egg b•x

UEA 17 Poets 2012

First published by Egg Box Publishing 2012
International © retained by individual authors

This book is sold subject to the condition that it shall not, by way of trade or otherwise, be lent, resold, hired out, stored in a retrieval system, or otherwise circulated without the publisher's prior consent in any form of binding or cover other than that in which it is published and without a similar condition including this condition being imposed on the subsequent purchaser.

A CIP record for this book is available from the British Library.

UEA 17 Poets 2012 is typeset in Caslon 10pt on 13pt leading with Din titles.

Printed and bound in the UK by CPI Antony Rowe Ltd.

Designed and typeset by Sean Purdy at The Ampersand.

Cover photography by Jerusha Green.

Proofread by Sarah Gooderson.

Distributed by Central Books
ISBN: 9780956928948

Acknowledgments

Thanks to the following for making this anthology possible:

The Malcolm Bradbury Memorial Fund, the Centre for Creative and Performing Arts at the University of East Anglia and The School of Literature, Drama and Creative Writing at UEA in partnership with Egg Box Publishing.

We'd also like to thank the following people:

Moniza Alvi, Jean Boase-Beier, Amit Chaudhuri, Andrew Cowan, William Fiennes, Giles Foden, Sarah Gooderson, Lavinia Greenlaw, Rachel Hore, Kathryn Hughes, Katie Konyn, Michael Lengsfield, Jean McNeil, Natalie Mitchell, Jeremy Page, Rob Ritchie, Helen Smith, Henry Sutton, George Szirtes, Val Taylor and Steve Waters.
Nathan Hamilton at Egg Box Publishing, Sean Purdy at The Ampersand and Jerusha Green.

Editorial team:
Linda Black
Natasha Broad
Gaynor Clements
Ella Chappell
Eluned Gramich
Tilly Lunken
Erin Meier
Judy O'Kane

Contents

Introduction
by Moniza Alvi, — *I*
Lavinia Greenlaw,
George Szirtes

Contributors
Alexander Allen — *12*
Mona Arshi — *18*
Ella Chappell — *26*
Stuart Charlesworth — *36*
Sophie Collins — *44*
Ned Denny — *52*
Laura Elliott — *58*
Beau Hopkins — *68*
Edwin Kelly — *78*
Timur Moon — *84*
Christopher Ogden — *94*
Amy Ramsay — *100*
Angus Sinclair — *108*
Matthew Spence — *116*
Eleanor Stewart — *124*
Cutter Streeby — *136*
Hayden Westfield-Bell — *146*

UEA Anthology 2012

Poetry

Introduction
by Moniza Alvi, Lavinia Greenlaw, George Szirtes

Alexander Allen
Mona Arshi
Ella Chappell
Stuart Charlesworth
Sophie Collins
Ned Denny
Laura Elliott
Beau Hopkins
Edwin Kelly
Timur Moon
Christopher Ogden
Amy Ramsay
Angus Sinclair
Matthew Spence
Eleanor Stewart
Cutter Streeby
Hayden Westfield-Bell

A course begins as strangers, moves towards a kind of community then spreads out again, though the networking world that is now our given may, for some, confirm and perpetuate that sense of community. Unless you are going to produce a manifesto of pooled ideas however, the temporary community of the class is not formed round ideologies or even practices. It is, rather, a kind of echo room where a voice may hear its own possible trajectory. The voices in this anthology are idiosyncratic and various as they should be.

It's interesting that while poetry in literary Scots has critical respectability, regional phonetic English doesn't, or rather not very often. So it is fascinating that Alexander Allen provides us with an example in his *Hunter's Mune*. In other poems, like *Menominee*, he examines an idea with grace, clarity and invention. How we get from the tower of ants to the last snow via the white shirt is one of those acts of poetry to which no licence ever applies.

Mona Arshi pursues the formation of intimacy, how it coalesces and fragments, and the shifting forces of containment and release: 'Here's my mouth,/hummingbird, linger there, and hold/my breath.' These poems are full of urgent imperatives, their images detonations of what cannot be said.

Ella Chappell's poems are formal, intellectual, scientific and marine. Her range is wide and while essentially lyrical, particularly in the sea and Venice poems, there is a sense that we are moving beyond description or personal feeling into an enquiry into the nature of things. So it is with *What it would would feel like* where clippings from *New Scientist* sit alongside snippets of song lyrics, as if to resituate us in a world where both worlds coexist.

As the title of Stuart Charlesworth's poems suggests, he is concerned with the understanding of the relationship between primal, elemental things and the consciousness that registers them. So in *path* a child is 'trailing behind his ghost-white father' much as the thin rain is 'stirring shadows from the water' while in *tree*, the tree itself with its 'arms/and a floor-length wool coat' is balanced against a man 'who talked less and less/and more quietly/who ate small meals/mostly drank water'. The two inhabit the same world, but on the tree's terms rather than the man's.

Sophie Collins's poems trace the complexities of sensation and perception that we find impossible to articulate: 'If I identify, it's only because/I've adopted this defence,/seeking out a substrate/on which to condense.' Her orchestrations of thought, image and found text start deep in the self and enlarge outwards through a concise surrealism.

Ned Denny's poems are often philosophical, sometimes mystical in nature and hard to carry off in a world generally not attuned to such things, but the range of his imagination and his formal control can present us with authoritative, highly wrought poems that exist in spaces of his own making. It is a poetry of ideas where a body of thought is brought to bear on specific experiences that are extended into something like hallucination.

Photography, desire, breath, and the body vying with its own representations, are central concerns in Laura Elliott's rapidly flowing, sinuous verse. The location is clear and quite specific, the details precise. In *A Compositional Arrangement (that) Persists*, a poem set around a meal, she tells us that 'you can/learn a lot about a person/from the way they use their instruments prepare their plate/compose their sentences' and moves towards 'the only rules': *'say something/silver say anything open we are so far/in hold your breath/she says and dives'*.

In an intricate sonnet sequence Beau Hopkins constantly undercuts the conventional lyricism of the love poem while retaining tenderness: 'I know/nothing really & want EVERYTHING/now to be personal, 'right' and touchable/like you in the dirty & lovely morning light.' His poems crackle with verbal agility and intellectual energy within their formal frames.

Edwin Kelly's refractive observations concentrate on surfaces and transparencies: water and glass. Birdsong is made concrete in analogy just as what seems clear or empty reveals itself, and ourselves, in the act of being described: 'when rain itself seems/a solidness of grief you dare not walk in/and the concrete it beats is a crying reply …'

Timur Moon fuses literary language: 'the sun blazing chromium', the colloquial: 'like bunting or something' and wordplay: 'we broke baguette'. He brings to a concern with verse structure and metre, a sense of the instability and the surrealism of life, life on the precipice, as embodied by the pest controllers stalking foxes 'halfway to the heavens', to where they'd been surviving, at the top of the Shard.

Christopher Ogden explores poetic form as emotional tension, from a *Star Wars* sestina in which the slippage of the end words exposes a fraying fantasy to the relentless rhyme of being stuck with the wrong person in a pub. His drive is towards an elusive conjunction of possibility and being in place: 'Then I sensed an opening, some belonging twisting in the blue.'

Amy Ramsay draws on the ballad and the fairytale to heighten and concentrate moments of profound unsettlement. Her poems are insistently musical and yet tautly measured and concise, a tension that amplifies the trapped presences and absences they address: 'Her second, born soft, flicked on flicked off/a third came slowly *E l i z a b e t h*.'

Angus Sinclair's assemblages from texts on logic have a deceptive playfulness: 'Some poets are surprised to discover they exist at all,/ some rectangles with equal and adjacent sides are squares.' They open out our ideas of how we make sense of the world, of words, of what we write and how we read. These themes extend into his poems about photographs and constellations to consider how we read the world.

by Moniza Alvi, Lavinia Greenlaw, George Szirtes

Matthew Spence's poems are about being on the move. So, in *Assen*, he takes a bus into town, registering flat greys and pinks, stops for a pizza by a deer park, gulps air, feels the 'invisible slips/of wind' and suddenly as he looks at his companion's face notes 'the stretch of all Europe' as well as the droplets on every blade of grass. It is the sheer presence, the physicality and uniqueness of phenomena within the all but incomprehensible largeness of the world that strike Spence time and again: the ground 'fat with water'.

Eleanor Stewart looks outwards towards other worlds, as well as to the more familiar one, and she inhabits other voices naturally and dramatically. Imaginative force and narrative reach combine with skills of sound-patterning and cadence: 'confined/within this barren saline sea; mute as a pillar of salt,/defined by my own concentrated, crystallising grief'.

Cutter Streeby's poems are marked by a strong pulse and a relish for language. They can rise to great contemplative and visionary power. An imaginary lizard is released onto the abdomen of a child or lover like 'a piece of your element coming unstitched'. Adventurous in shape and lineation, his poems can be playful, as well as urgent.

Hayden Westfield-Bell evokes threatening, elemental powers often set against the domestic or quotidian, in poems that explore their own sharp inner logic. Stanzas of short, measured lines build to, and contain, jagged shifts and explosions: 'think of you,//wandering home/wrapped in plastic,/bags on your back//banging against/your hips in that vicious/falling-down.'

These poets bring their own backgrounds and impulses with them to the course. They develop as they individually need to, but in the sustaining companionships and intelligence fellow poets can provide. They inhabit the echo room of the moment. Let that room be wide and high, then let it echo.

MA, LG, GS
June 2012

Alexander Allen

Hunter's Mune
Menominee
Mekico®
Nashi Pear

Hunter's Mune

For John Kett, 1912 – 2010

Thur be hunter's mune booi,
pitchin up twin sails o' far owl mill.
How mellow booi, how plumply filled
is that paale haarvest pumpkin,
that even in this lairt hoor still,
all wood baards be rightly baitin –

robin, rook, linnet, spaarrow
all anoint this bull's nune sun
who blooms as white boon flushed
with pinkish maarrow. Yet owld fast bor,
keep thine wick a moment more;
for now thur noight be blowin clare

and when wind sighs on baarley's ear
bop down son, keep sorf yoor tread
and fix yoor eyes on sheeted snow,
for this'n hunter's mune will show
where footprints o' roe deer brim
like thimbles blue and full wi' shadow.

by Alexander Allen

Menominee

Once I remember, in math
I was thinking how numbers
stacked on the page
were like a tower of ants,
the way they pass
with dumb practice
through each black mandible
these wavering fragments
we all know would crush us
were they scaled to the equivalent size,
when you turned

to give me the note
and I saw how the white paper
creased like the white shirt
stretched across your back
(*ketapanen* it said)
and how the rain came then,
drumming on the roof
of the science annex,
and went tailing across pines,
arriving at the lake's edge
where winter's last snow
dimpled.

Mekico®

We are thrilled to present
an intriguingly new coffee
which only by a slow gentle
roasting each bean
in the traditional rotary drum
is a unique advantage!

"Drinking Mekico® Coffee
I was feeling a new man
containing all the excellent qualities
of men
and none of the impurities!"

The superior balanced flavours
are so formed in the beans,
air cooled for perfect equilibrium
at the clean high altitudes
and in the most natural sunlight
and weather conditions.

"Mekico® Coffee is true!
It transforms the spirit.
I enjoy mine
with a handful of dried fruit
and a thin cream."

Drink Mekico® Coffee
and in a small white cup
you are conveyed to the joyful
life, where richness flourishes!

by Alexander Allen

"I have visited Mexico
to see the pomegranate flowers
in the sacred gardens
of mission churches
and Mekico® Coffee is the flavour
that keeps me in this memory."

Nashi Pear

Although it has been grown
to be beautiful,
do not make an ornament of it
as you might a candle, or a fossil,
but take a sharp blade
and cut through the centre –
a clean white disc.

Hold it up to the light,
and teach your baby nephew
sleeping in the sway
of your arms,
the crook of your branches,
the meaning of the word
translucent.

....

Alexander Allen graduated from the University of East Anglia in 2009, having studied American Literature with Creative Writing. As part of his degree, he spent a year in rural Illinois, where he met and was taught by Chicago and blues poet Tyehimba Jess. He developed a feel for historical/narrative poetry, using extracts from Einstein's diary in an early collection. On his return to the UK, he followed up his experience in the States with a collection of poems centring on Chicago, and specifically the Great Fire of 1873, for which he won the 2009 UEA Year Abroad Dissertation Prize. Since graduating, he splits his time between London and Italy, teaching English as a second language.

by Alexander Allen

Mona Arshi

Hummingbird
Ticking
The Wakening
Woman at window
Notes on Ceremonials

Hummingbird

Ask the stems in the glass to bend. Let
Your fingers fly, a momentary grasp then

  slip into spaces, surge in and out of folds
  where breasts begin to curve and rise.

Be God. Press your curing skin to mine,
dissolve and pronounce me. Let my eyes

  fallout and embed in the carpet, rooting.
  Let my hands arrange the air for you,

braiding. Reluctant sun at the window, open
your eyes burn through the dense haze with

your severe love. Slides open the bone-zip of
my spine, anoint each rigid peak. Take my

limbs and fold me over. Here's my mouth,
hummingbird, linger there, and hold
my breath.

by Mona Arshi

Ticking
i.m. Diane Pretty

They lead me (nervous and suited) to the
living room. She's all peachy toed and rimmel-red
mouthed smiles. Machines grind and wink, but
if you listen with care you can hear that her body
is ticking, then cracking and oozing out her liquid
life, onto the carpeted floor. She is now an interpreter
of silence, can read the walls' unease, reveal why the
silvery sounds of dawn rasp just for her.
She is aware that she is being edited, imperceptibly
nibbled by tiny fish, and contracting down to this
verse, this line, in the papers "I am Diane – Help me."

The Wakening

I woke and my arm had died in the dark
I shook it awake,
waiting for pink plush to resurface.
You always said I had a tendency to catastrophise everything,
a dropped stitch in the brain's manufacture.
You sat close and I watched you sketch an incoherent moon,
it was as intimate as skin
        or language

It was as intimate as skin
        or language
You sat close and I watched you sketch an incoherent moon
A dropped stitch in the brain's manufacture
You always said I had a tendency to catastrophise everything
waiting for pink plush to resurface
I shook it awake
I woke and my arm had died in the dark.

by Mona Arshi

Woman at window

It's Decemberish and raining.
The kiss you left on my eyelashes
is dying down.
Everything has changed.

The window shows me clouds
that have not altered,
and the sky, is jaundiced yet still
refuses to stain light.

Meanwhile, your morning progresses,
and under some other light you're sitting,
tapping out data, or smoking outside
a doorway.

Down below a man continues sweeping,
collecting fallen things.

I contemplate window glass,
quietly fracturing on its own terms.

Notes on Ceremonials

~

You will sit as naked as a bird,

as primitive as the first bird,
with whom you share the same
enigmatic bone.

~

Your mouth, your mouth, emits
a soft straight whistle,
and your tongue is clicking,
sort of interpreting the air

~

We will practise the art of calligraphy,
Fix angled lines on your wings,
on my breast, on the soles of my feet.

~

When I coax you onto my fingers,
You will part and flower in my palm.

~

Dear, quailing thing, don't lose your nerve
I know the hours are sweetening too much and the light can be
brutal.
This room is vast and open-blue,
it's bluer than any eye could bear.

by Mona Arshi

The world is a small globe,
it hurts my eyes too, too bright.
Fly! Dissolve us both to liquid light.

~

Mona Arshi was born in West London into a Sikh Punjabi family. She worked for several years as a human rights lawyer in the UK. Her poem 'Hummingbird' won first prize in the *Magma* poetry competition in 2012. As well as crafting poems, Mona is working on her first novel based around where she grew up.

by Mona Arshi

Ella Chappell

Quantum
The Golden
Icebergs
Mrs
Venice
What it would feel like

Quantum

You want to walk in the dark garden of the eye of the deer looking at you.
— Tim Lilburn

You want to walk in the dark path
of the quantum logic compelling you.

Under the wake of the mind
you travel at a hurtling rate
the precise speed of meetings
eatings codeine nicotine blush red
amber green after the traffic jam
after the sangria after the caffeine
keep on, the idea is not to think

Or find you standing stock still in the woods
looking for the deer with your brother
among the bluebells somewhere
the forms breathe in spite of their absence.
How fast do you travel in this lung land?
the lines of light and shade;
the trees that try to decode you.

by Ella Chappell

The Golden

O
Shell
Or
Bird turn
Deft and bright
Right to the centre
Of things. Set your feet to the world
As chemicals hurrying to the brain's synapses.

Did you stop in the flowing of the crowd to wait and watch the starlings demonstrate their mathematics? Did you look a moron just standing there? Did you know that their movements can be exactly mimicked by computer graphic simulations assuming that each bird will stay equidistant from all others around it? A group of starlings is called a murmuration of starlings, a filth of starlings. Or an affliction of starlings, it certainly didn't feel that way, did it? Bubbles will naturally minimise their surface area in order to be optimally efficient. In the air, free from all else, they form a perfect sphere. The concept of fractals allows the twig to appear as beautiful and complete as the tree itself. The starlings giggle at you too, standing there, head to the sky, wondering at the numbness of numbers.

Icebergs

We are measured in miles.
We are the thoughts you had
but didn't voice, even to yourself.
We are marbled, cold,
sometimes sculptural, sometimes
tables to nothing in particular,
going nowhere in particular.

Homeward bound, stuffed with wool from Tasmania,
sailing beneath the tip of Argentina,
the Eden Holme encountered head winds that forced
her to run considerably south of the ordinary track.
She got amongst the ice.
Passing one day between daybreak and dark
ninety large bergs or icelands.

We are the shine in the dark water.
We are the phosphenes behind your eyes.
Here we are the only things that waves have to hit.
We would be stone if it were not for our
rainbows and double visions.

I was sitting in my cabin at night
when there was a great commotion on deck,
and running up I found the ship bearing down
upon a huge iceberg which had just loomed
in her path from the darkness.
One crewman's face I will never forget.

We are crests of light frozen to stillness.
The act of ice is simple as love.
We transmute white into jittering hues,
We melt gently with the fish.

by Ella Chappell

When I had grasped the situation
and given the necessary orders,
the remainder of the crew sprung to it,
and we succeeded in just skimming along
the side of the berg,
which, in the moonlight, was lightened up,
and drew from me an involuntary exclamation.

And that's when we saw him.
Our miniscule geometries, our transparent
prisms and crystals glittered.
We passed like a window in which his
almost-reflection hummed.
We, no colours, all colours,
slowly met the ship.
Could one on the other side
see his eye, distorted,
as though through glass?

Mrs

Sometimes I imagine that you're here
walking down the street towards me
making some inexplicable arrangement with autumn.
Your silver birch gait
heavy step in boots folding out
like a collapsing old rose.

You don't see me and I
                  stop
                  as if your name
                  spoken aloud by my voice
                  stands before my path.

But you carry on past me
because your eyes are blinded by
the Bay of Biscay, Eden Holme, and
like a bubble, your own multiplying contours of joy,
that made me seasick.
Weightless in the only ways that matter,
you are taken by the wind and away.

Sometimes I imagine that you're here.
A white feather on a lavender bush is
a single hair of mine caught on your lip.

by Ella Chappell

Venice

As smoke meeting a ceiling
the sea presses up to the ship.

The fat, expressionless faces of clouds
freckled with birds, push down.

In the vacuum of between, he stands almost breathless with desire
at the bow he watches the sea. He is thirteen and a half.

He lets his palm prickle across the wooden side.
They've told him Venice should soon be in sight but the ocean is stubborn.

It refuses even the sun that dives hopelessly into its cold arms.
Touches of pinks of purples ripen the sky around the belly.

The ocean waits to engulf it as a Venus trap yielding to press over a fly.

Darkness. The ocean remains open mouthed but silent
roaring in whispers, wide as the sky but too full for stars,

lapping at the sides of the ship in thorns of dew
explaining slowly the reason why he can't stop looking.

What it would feel like
(a poem sourced from electro lyrics and a *New Scientist* article)

Blackhole

Quiet heart, it's a quiet heart, it's a quiet heart.
If you're falling in feet first, gravity at your head is much weaker than at your feet.
Hollow chest, it's a hollow chest, it's a hollow chest.
It also affects the light falling in around you - light from above your head is stretched out and shifted to the red end of the spectrum. Eventually it gets red-shifted into nothingness, so your whole view will be squeezed into a horizontal ring.
I don't want to be Woody Allen in 'Hannah and her Sisters' making a deal with god.
Close to the singularity, it appears that the entire three-dimensional universe is being crushed into a two-dimensional surface.
Somedays – white, sunless – the way hired light falls on a table, a wall, nearly without thinking, I know it.
Is there information loss? Is there information loss?

Wormhole

Once you reach its inner horizon, you see an infinitely-energetic flash of light from the outside world containing an image of the entire history of the universe.
Wait, synthesisers fade out, (whispering) yeah fuck my life, (a laugh,) this hurts so bad, this hurts my body, my arms.
but the visualisation assumes you have superpowers to survive it.
(A woman's voice) wait, (a man's voice) wait.
The flow of space turns around and you start to accelerate back outward. Instead of falling inward, space falls outwards at a speed faster than light.
You wander into the bedroom. You're drunk, we've done this before. You stumbled over like three seconds later and kick your boots on to the floor.
Soon you experience another flash of radiation, this time containing a picture of the entire future of the universe.

by Ella Chappell

When beginning and end are interchangeable, I'd like to sign off the way I signed in, with innocence.
This time, a new universe appears, containing an image of its entire past.
My love for you will surely be the death of me.

Ella Chappell was born in 1990 in South Manchester and went on to read English Literature and Creative Writing at UEA, graduating in 2011. Her poetry has been featured on numerous online journals and she is currently UK Editor of student art webzine *StudentAtLarge*. She doesn't know where she's going next but she's excited.

by Ella Chappell

Stuart Charlesworth

path
tree —
fence
two ghazals: versions after Federico Garcia Lorca
the moon explains sunsets to the sun

path

    perhaps you should not have come
                    wandering along me –

      the light from the sky
    intends to explore you

      it has been busy since dawn
              making arrangements

     as it falls through the trees
    so it shall through you

up ahead in your way
           is a thin rain
    stirring shadows from the water
                    that runs at your side
    and making the day work harder
                        to find any colour
       in the wet sides of leaves
                  and soaked bark
     but those that do show through –
   muddy greens
          yellows and browns
are as vivid
      and distorted
as the memories they will invoke –

you will remember
    when you were younger
      and would walk
           in woods
               like these
                     alone

      look! here is a robin for company

    and when you are ready to continue
        a pair of swans
              will land
   on the ground in front of you

       their bodies will unfold
    and reshape
        as two silent humans –
      a child
           trailing behind
      his ghost-white father

                and though i might like to
                      i cannot turn
      and take you along by another way

by Stuart Charlesworth

                                                            tree –

       you appeared to stand peacefully
       till i found the remains
                                    of an old factory wall –
                     pulled to bricks and damp dust
                              during the slow
                                        creeping searches
                                                    of your roots

       i want to know why you've done that
       but can't
                see how you work
                  when i stare
                            close at long branches
                          and smooth straight bark
                                 i think of arms
                                      and a floor-length wool coat

       and if i try to imagine
                            your tree-seed floating here
       falling
              then shooting a sapling
                                thickening
                 i see a man
                           instead
                      who talked less and less
                                      and more quietly
                            who ate small meals
                                        mostly drank water
                                awake
                                    worried
                                        and out walking in the night

       were you looking
                for something hard
                              to break apart
                                        and break apart
                              until it could not be broken any more?

                              are you drawing-up the fragments
                                      slowly
                                            becoming stronger?

       tree
             i tell myself this
       is not how things are
       i should look at what's here
                  and i find i've been standing
                                    next to you for so long
                           my legs are hard to bend

Assorted Poetry

fence

The houses, though small cramped and poor, are built from carefully laid bricks and aspire to keep that neatness. Fence by comparison looks wild. He runs within the first of the rangy trees, as if he's wandered out of place. If fence was ever tame he's a feral thing now.

The parents that live in the small houses expect him to stop their little-ones from straying close to the water. But they climb over him, break him and trample him flat. Fence doesn't mind, he understands kids, and how awake it feels to be out by yourself.

two ghazals: versions after Federico Garcia Lorca

ghazal: The Duende

How has the flood overcome you this evening? The Duende.
Who let the tempest escape with its terrible raging? The Duende.

Who plucks the flower of gold from your heart
when the night is so hot that stars begin fainting? The Duende.

The grass and leaves chit-chat and cows gossip
about murdered worms, but who is translating? The Duende.

The corpse of the diva; who tarnished her dress
and makes sure the teeth in her skull are still shining? The Duende.

And who carries struggling night in his arms
to a broken asylum for time every morning? The Duende.
Do you wish to know his hunger for dark planets,
because the secrets of your waist are calling the Duende?

Then you must freely give your innermost self
like soft cactus flesh. Are you ready? He is waiting – The Duende.

by Stuart Charlesworth

ghazal: Of the Sea

I would dream the sleep of the boy from the high sea;
the boy who wanted his heart to lie on the sea.

I'd dream like an apple – but not in a churchyard
full of those lucky enough not to die out at sea.

I don't want to learn the methods that grass
makes its martyrs by, nor those of the sea;

that the dead cannot bleed but will call out for water –
those putrid mouths of theirs cry like the sea;

and don't talk of the moon with a serpent's mouth
at work before dawn, in the sky above the sea.

But no one should think that I've died
if I sleep for a second, or century by the sea

there'd be gold at my lips and my friend would be
the wind that flies in off the sea.

Cover me with a veil before the dawn,
its armies of ants terrify me more than the sea.

And water my shoes till they're slippery-wet
so the scorpion's claw cannot bite like cold spray from the sea.

Because I'd dream the sleep of the apples,
to hold off the earth with a lullaby like the sea

and I'd live with that strange and dark boy
who wanted his heart cut high on the sea.

the moon explains sunsets to the sun

as the day begins
        the sun speaks –

i move slowly this morning
as if shuffling through my ablutions
                  in a voluminous dressing-gown –
  i spread more colour than white-light

    so the moon is still visible
        like mist
            trying to form
                a broken circle

                        the moon says

              after you passed the tree-line
                            leaving
        the last lighter blue
                      running behind you
    the dark washed in
                      and i appeared brighter

        but alone
                and suddenly felt so high
                afraid to move for falling
                  my small reflection
              on the water
                      shaking

by Stuart Charlesworth

another day awakens
the sun speaks again –

i realise it's a new morning
        only when the moon explains
                          what happened
        after i last went away

    but sometimes
             damp-towel clouds
                        block my view

        and she is just a bodiless voice
                          adrift

                          that voice says

      they wandered across
                in ones and twos in the darkness
        and while everybody slept
                  they formed this mob
    now they can't decide whether to rain
                  or race back to the sea –

    do you remember
        at the end of yesterday
                there were only a few of them?
        and how the reds
             refracted through their shapes?

                    they were still glowing
                              minutes after you had gone

                         but when there is no one to talk to
                                         the sun thinks —
for me
       this is still morning
          it must be night-time for the moon

              but i can't believe in a difference
                              between those two states
                   — unless i am hearing her speak

       how would i explain this to her?
              if i were to say —
              i am the sun!
                        an event of fire!
                                   with the laws of space-time
                    perceptibly bending around me —
                                        it would not move her
closer

                    if i change
                         the way *i* am thought of
                    what will happen to the moon?

....

Stuart Charlesworth previously studied International Politics and International History at The University of Wales, Aberystwyth, and Learning Disabilities Nursing at the University of East Anglia. He lives in Norwich and works as a nurse for people with learning difficulties. He is involved in the running of a creative writing and translation workshop at UEA, which he co-created.

by Stuart Charlesworth

Sophie Collins

Please write clearly:
Substance
From *Nolita*
The answers
From *The hidden messages in water*
Suburb
From the window of a moving train

Please write clearly:

Upon waking, I reached instinctively for my chest where I expected to find the surgeon's incision. It was in fact much lower down – an inch or so above the navel, and really very small. I noticed a jar had been placed on the bedside unit, presumably so that I should inspect the contents out of morbid curiosity. Smaller than expected, they were no larger than bees and darker than damp soil. Having ascertained that the drugs had not had much effect, the nurse discharged me later that day. By this time the contents of the jar were wasting visibly; some resting motionless on the base, others fluttering despondently against its sides. They did not react well to daylight, and would have perished immediately if touched. On my way through the car park I saw them being loaded into a vehicle along with hundreds of other similar jars. I spotted mine almost instantly, nestled between a jar of filthy water, and another that contained a single glowing pebble.

by Sophie Collins

Substance

I had been reading about ancient belief
in 'upper' and 'lower' waters, how the former
represents potential — a cloud or a contrail —
and the latter the actual: a lake or canal.
Coming across 'skull-water', I said it aloud.

But you asked about condensation,
where steam and rain came in.
'Why not call a cloud a cloud?
Why complicate the thing?'

from **Nolita**

The property always feared her comrades' eyes.
The eyes that never winked. That cannot accept becoming.
Cannot advise becoming.

The method cannot be extracted – becoming the enemy.
Criticism is the speaker's quickstep, the dirty typist.
Define becoming.

The science of public understanding of private interest.
Picture philosophy and her problems –
An embraceable region becoming the commons of the face.

The audience wants what the audience gets.
A garden comes into use. Some follow the montage.
Public choice – a model worth the arts subjects. Worth.

Worth the science.
Burning locations
character the private.

by Sophie Collins

The answers
with Sam Riviere

The patrol car comes to a stop in a sleepy neighbourhood
of small, earth-coloured homes.

Sebastian rallied:
'We're more like radio receivers than you'd like to admit.

The chances are that if a simulation can be created,
we are living in it.'

Away from the vents, life is very sparse indeed
in this part of the world.

Jupiter's heart is dissolving,
melting, collapsing, divorcing.

The research, he says,
is just getting going.

The answers are to remain sealed in an envelope
until further notice, for everyone's protection.

Source: http://www.newscientist.com/section/science-news

from The Hidden Messages in Water

Simple Prisms

Formed by an invasion of air
or a sudden updraught into cooler elevations,
water takes to some particle of dirt,
is carried to the top or bottom of a cloud
and held there.

If I identify, it's only because
I've adopted this defence,
seeking out a substrate
on which to condense.

Suburb

Suburb that friends come and leave
Suburb that friends come and leave
but that
that is enough.
No matter, Suburb.

[Suburb fierceness at interviewer]

Suburb, happiness isn't based in properties.

Suburb I'm alone.
Suburb I'm bleak.

by Sophie Collins

From the Window of a Moving Train

Suddenly I am struck by the stillness of horses.
I miss my turn in the game. Outside are objects,
we must spot them. The rules are not complex.

But is a rainbow worth more than a cloud?
A church equal to ten burnt-out sheds?
How much for a flag, a scarecrow or a swarm of bees?

A couple in love, a couple not in love, a tree stump, a crime-scene?
An upturned rowboat, a child's kite, a face at a window?
A fist-fight? Lost money? Perfect light? A girl, running?

Sophie Collins grew up in Holland and moved to London in 2007 to study Creative Writing at Goldsmiths College. Her poems have appeared or are forthcoming in *Mercy, Rising, Clinic* and *SSYK*. She will begin a PhD in Poetry and Translation at Queen's University Belfast this year.

by Sophie Collins

Ned Denny

Words
Annunciation
Dense Mayan Traffic (Omphalos)
Helix
Room
Rip

Words

after Charles Baudelaire

When into this bolted, shit-smeared crack den
pale dawn extends her roseate light
she starts to work a subtle revenge:
the angel within you half opens one eye.

For creatures like us, cast down by thought,
the deep blue of the unseen mesosphere
exerts an abyssal and summoning force;
whilst she, quiet goddess, her countenance clear,

gilds the wretched debris of a session –
the bitten wraps, charred foil and wire-stuffed glass –
and shimmers in front of my stony gaze.

Daybreak yellows a plastic lighter's flame;
similarly, the articulate sun
is put to shame by the brilliance of our hearts.

by Ned Denny

Annunciation

She is attacked one bookish day
for no discernible reason
by a beautifully dressed man.

She admires the velvet collar
of his elegant coat
as he launches himself at her with both hands.

She observes the stitching of his boots
as he kicks her
in the face with all his might.

O he left me kneeling in a garden,
my hands filled with blood
and each dark cell alight.

Dense Mayan Traffic (Omphalos)

You put your head into the hive
and nothing's quite the same again.
Our flesh is light, our flesh is wild,

we are not who we think we are.
We teem with undiscovered stars.

Nature winks through a veil of names.

Helix

Sometimes you see them everywhere, dragons.
　　　– Matthew Francis, Dragons

I am the ancient one,
adorner of the cooling rock,

genius of the newborn seas,
artificer of air.

Coiled inside the cell's brine
I plotted rains and monsters,

have imagined everything
that ever sensed this garden

whose green is my invention
too. I am the buried gleam

that will not be believed in,
a celestial animator

hidden in my own cartoon,
the eyes behind the eyes

of scientist, beech and house-fly.
My origins are beyond you,

my shining scales the library
Alexandria could never be.

I am the educator,
the programmer of Snake TV

by Ned Denny

(the note from the depths,
mind's electricity,

this *alien, point-blank, green and actual*
light transmitting continually).

Room

When thirty spokes put their heads together

or clay is coaxed into a form and baked,
you have a wheel that flashes round a hole
and a pot whose treasure is an empty space.
We raise a roof and four solid walls
to build a house but we occupy the air;
our being in the world depends upon

mastering the use of what isn't there.

(Tao Te Ching, xi)

Rip

You are just about to turn for home,
back to the chickens strutting in the dirt
and village gossip and a tonguelash from her,

when something in the silence holds you.
It is a quiet composed of many sounds
(each one as small as it is clear)

that call and call to a distant stillness
our dialect has no words for.
You fall to the grass. The hour's a song

to empty the skull, moving in the giant sky
and men disguised as mountain pines.
It is as though you have been asleep,

as if you have stumbled out of time.
The dwarves are gone. Their dreamless faces
leer from the rocks and the rocky clouds,

down at the trees whose ascent is music.
You are just about to turn for home.
The minutes pass like seasons, centuries.

....

Ned Denny was born in London and has been writing poetry since the age of 16. He has been art critic of the *New Statesman* and drum & bass correspondent for *Muzik* magazine, has reviewed science books in *The Observer* and delivered letters for Royal Mail. His poems have been published in several magazines including *PN Review*.

by Ned Denny

Laura Elliott

So Much Rain for Days
Heinrich-Roller Straße, 26
A Compositional Arrangement (that) Persists
It is Always about the Distant Claims on Appearances

So Much Rain for Days

trapped taking pictures
in our one room studio you wanted
        to balance eggs
                on my eyelids
cool as fingertips and strip my clothes off
why did you want to do it that way
        what could you see
                it was raining outside maybe
the rain had stopped then you plugged in
all the lamps bare bulbs crisping
        their residue of dust
                their orange-white glare
angled down on me from
the two chairs the table the
        white-tiled window ledge
                I always thought I would fall off
when I sat on the lip and smoked
I leaned so far so far out I could almost
        touch the leaves of the tree
                that sounded so clearly like rain
every morning I would think it was rain again
rain again always rain but not always
        so I learned to lean
                outside to touch the rain-tree
in the courtyard one hand holding
my little glass of coffee and it became
        a ritual I didn't think
                you even noticed nearly
all summer long I did it every
single morning but one of those days
        you wanted me to lie down
                on the parquet with no clothes on

by Laura Elliott

and balance eggs on my eyelids
so that you could take a photograph
        I only wanted you to see
                that I could do it I could lie
quite still and listen to the rain-tree
and feel all the lamps on me tensing
        your breath on my body
                and nothing fell or was broken
nothing happened except
for one morning I couldn't see
        the ledge or the leaves
                or whether it was raining

Heinrich-Roller Straße, 26

go outside
the sun wants you
whole not in patches caught
through the window everyone
is waiting watching you
interior standing nude
in the office across the courtyard
I can't help but be distracted gaze
through the sunlight refractions
reveal yourself to us
bathed in glass

> *I want you to*
> *see me mirrored open*
> *sweeping leaves into the frame*
> *or wider windows in my window*
> *I want you brief and incoherent*
> *as a green vase either one end*
> *or the other of the sill*
> *glance up please show me how*
> *you can resist the light lash blinds*
> *across the pane*

quiet after rain
the foyer floods with puddles swaying
on marble tiles
sunlight glints on windows dipped
in water and your window
filled always with you above
your body reflected back on itself
through glass-edged outlines placed
and replaced by the swing
of a window the persistence
of a lime green vase

by Laura Elliott

is this anything
to care for the way endlessly
I pick and put and redefine the long days
with surfaces leading into skin
this column responds
I am giving you versions
of distance here you can touch this vase
if you open just right there
we share this overlapping
glass with glass

can you feel me
trace your window onto mine
does the light intensify
in a sudden rush of contours
realigned did you forget to breathe did you
forget how easy it can be
to tip into another room hold
space around a figure
holding on to you look over here
is something you can grasp if you reach
we can leave here yet

A Compositional Arrangement (that) Persists

bones bristle like whiskers
in your teeth she is delighted
the plates match little blue waves
    pulsing between you

the construction of a meal
one table two chairs the table
is glass/wood and assembled
on top are various plates full
of foods with rinds and crusts
and bones and furs foods
that require utensils precision
and care to unwrap you can
learn a lot about a person
from the way they use their
instruments prepare their plate
compose their sentences

saucers stacked on the lid
of the table a tank fish float on air
rearrange the dishes fish spin
    on discs of ocean

but if the table is made of
i) wood then details such as
the colour of the plates
and the clarity of the food
the tonal qualities of the plate
arrangement gradually alter

by Laura Elliott

the atmosphere of the table
(think about subtle shade
variations draw attention
to particular areas dynamics
connections between people)

    place the plates below
      the table blue flares through glass
like gasps of breath
      beneath the surface

and if the table is made of
ii) glass then the plates are also
to be made of glass and
the gentle digestion used
to reveal _____
beneath the table or this be
enacted more slowly and
the plates are made of porcelain
and same as above (i) attention
to colour moving softly into
(ii) skin beneath glass for
the practice these are the only rules

    below the foam frills say something
    silver say anything open we are so far
in hold your breath
    she says and dives

It is Always about the Distant Claims on Appearances

      what is it about the journey that holds you
        so lightless shuddering into nowhere
clenching dark inside the car
even the stars
in their own way deny us
        portioned by glass fixed
        on the strained horizon

              there are gaps in everything
              you show me in your vests in your eyes
                  in your letters
                I fix these shapes in pictures
                or make semblances from stones
              how can you doubt
              that specificity

      we have lost each other driving through
        farmlands closed fields breathing fibres of gold
russet leaves the textures
of everything we can't see
richer on the skin imagine
        being wrapped in this night long enough
        to feel its ripening body

              I want to make it possible to want
              something (un)true I want you to be
                  (un)sure of me
                this drawing was (not) taken
                from life this stone is (a replica)
              painted to resemble that stone (why
              do you) believe me

by Laura Elliott

   go back to the wheels faltering
    was it nothing
at all your face emptied maybe
a hint of dial lights
but you were not there
    do not lay claim do not lay anything
    down we could share

      you say this is (not)
      the way mornings should feel
       we are noticing surfaces
       and hurting them testing the limits of
       (y)our perception did you see did you
      (want to) see here underneath
      are fingerprints

  your hand in my lap in starlight no
   we knew nothing of stars
perhaps a struggle so sure of ourselves
eventually light rushing yellow
unbounded out and
   up and everything
   hurtling unclasped

      the difference (in touch)
      weighs nothing but
       your voice hollows nearing
       truth (I feel) your difference
       drawing deep
      from its stone (here
      is what we know)

Laura Elliott graduated from Norwich University College of the Arts in 2009, and subsequently won the Café Writers Norfolk Commission. Her first pamphlet *Bridge* was published by Gatehouse Press in 2010, and her work has since featured in various publications, including *The Best British Poetry 2011* collection, published by Salt.

by Laura Elliott

Beau Hopkins

Metamorphosis
…et uxor.
Directions
Down and Out at the Woolwich Arsenal
From *Sonnets from B to A:*
    Can't See So Well
    Wakey Wakey
    And Then A Trial
    Meteorological Love
    Postcard From A Beach
    Old Draff, New Draff
Blakeney Marsh

Metamorphosis

avec puces ou non
  — Corbière

Oi you, centipede! That's what they called me
— *Slug!* — on my first day at school. *Hello worm!*
Try as I might, they wouldn't change their minds,
so in my daydreams I subjected them
to tortures and interrogation techniques
used by the Gestapo. But fourteen came:
a turning point. I stopped myself from hating
them from afar; instead I spoke to God,
feigned indifference, and started wearing black.
Then something strange happened. In the street
two young boys (I was older now, a prefect)
paused. As they observed me, I saw their cheeks
hackle and contort with horror. So I
scuttled away on my one hundred legs.

by Beau Hopkins

... et uxor.

I make his dinner and then we have sex.
Sometimes we read my books; either he'll grimace
or laugh hysterically. And once, for variation,
I threw away the Scrabble and daubed HEAVEN
in mauve ink on the living room wall. Tim
said nothing – just turned and let me loose his tie.
My star-sign said *You can't go on like this*
and *Try something new!* So one day in town
I obtained a strange concoction from the chemist
(having no intention, at that stage, to kill)
which I mixed in with his pear mousse. *Evening dull!*
(He called me *dull* not *darling*, as he sat down ...)
Imagine now my ecstasy – my joy! – as I
witness his toupée grow claws and scratch him!

Directions
i.m. Juan Rulfo

Follow me. At the top of this hill you
find, between the matted plaques of dried blood –

left there after their most recent *visit* –
a path. This leads away from the flies

and heat, the grunt of artillery, the shrieks
of women and the whining of shot dogs.

You will have a good view, when you go up.
You will find your way from there, by the smoke.

Down and Out at the Woolwich Arsenal

The Grand Store, so-called bomb-keep, burst now;
guns peacock through the wharves, goitrous with pleasing
lack of use; performance of obsolescence
where crows heave and stone light wrinkles the Thames.

Across the water, those who wrought them
watch from the bank. They are like shadows that watch
fire gnaw on tinder. Or are they like time – open and cool?
They, too, are as feelingly wrought as ancient stoves!

by Beau Hopkins

From Sonnets From B To A

They seemed Others, but are We

                              – Traherne

Can't See So Well

What I live in: you, us, and ALL-TIME. Also
my abandonment to blindness & with that
a new, lush definition. Now watch my mouth
give breath, riding the static
ion-flustered curve that comets from the bed –
the universe jailed in imagination:
the fungible nature of my 'just' response
REAL, as required. So it's true: parabolas stroke
our cross-nine equation silkwork to form
co-efficients for you 'n' me. But my wish
is for you, only: because I know
nothing really & want EVERYTHING
now to be personal, 'right' and touchable
like you in the dirty & lovely morning light.

Wakey Wakey

O SUN. Your heat is such a nice alarm,
breathing so politely on the skin.
And when it jigs, I feel it dance and burn
deep in the blood, all wavy & alive with a
wild whiteness. Eyes, go back in. I want to feel
as the heartbeats come, barely touching,
her dream-movements, like little, awkward falls
in silence, shaking out the hush of our
bedsit-cum-paradise.
Yeah but God, ignore all that crap.
I used to impress you. Now all my skill
lingers & goes cold, dimming like a ceiling light.
But still I am, even futuring every
thing, present to you, you & in you.

And Then A Trial

Now to be decided: by a judge; PROOF, & pro-
cess of recess seeking (shall we say)
leave before flight? Thank you m'lud. Or otherwise
in principle grounded? Ah but that's so
ab initio, so grown dim, so ab-
dicated & insofaras. I feel no
contact in the touch, no touch
in my nameless, blindly named, naked
HUNGER. Dressed you who did then?
Tell me now, now it is not.
O life. Press & abuse this
button. Pray out: out of never; out of what;
what I am & out of all other
things like love's seasons as the green year rounds.

by Beau Hopkins

Meteorological Love

HAIL – that's praise from the vile weather.
Achoo! – like *that*. But how I look to & at
you, yes dripping like the windscreen in the rain –
is this lens just some other guy's
used residue? Someone said
'a glue of words' – that was good, expressive
but wrong: they are so much quicker
now, than that; the way they rush up your breath
in rhythm, which is its own
thing now. That DROP just flattened us, these hills
to a dead stop: I can see NOTHING
useful. But still, into this void I
pour my unclean song, a floodtide of love:
those ravens, this night our jewelled dearth.

Postcard From A Beach

Seriously, what judge could picture this and not
cry out like the first TIME, tongue flinching like the
ply of the swift's wing as it twists and dies
down, tearing the bone & throat?
So we walk: above the waves, whose loneliness
is the old mackerel boat crusted by the salt
& by her conduct. Say again? Oh much
obliged m'lud. Now we hear: part of the
PROOF of any thing is how you stress it;
so wind struts here, picking up stones,
then falls asleep beneath the gravel coverlet
which approaches with each line of foam, harshly
by & large, in favour of you, my un
stressed soft point – quick breath – and the heart stops.

Old Draff, New Draff

What I live in: you, us & all-time – a cloud
scudding & shoved by time, us the shadow.
Huh. I see the garage door is shut
& the trees have ground to a halt. You could say
all time's just a matter of time, of course, so stop
rehearse, or do what you like, *I'll* never stop
as you creep back to bed from the window
all frigid with your dream. And the sheets,
like the moon you rode in on,
icy & stiff. One more … what? Lip, eye, a burning word?
No. Just look up again and admire it –
nobody, I mean nobody at all –
night's odd like that: it comes, like understanding,
sudden to the heart, & flowers us with stars.

by Beau Hopkins

Blakeney Marsh

And now the rain felt-tips the shifting pages
of the reedbeds, squeaky tonight with raucous
mating season sounds – egret, meadow pipit &
widgeon in there somewhere, hooting & clacky.
Later, as the chicks hatch, shearing the air,
their cheeps will prick you like a needlehead
in cloth, even when alone in some quiet & neat
bungalow. But now – now the rain gets in there
darkening it all, rummaging like a drunk
surgeon, crying Dinnertime! and botching the
handiwork. So first my fingers try to itch at
you, feeling you hidden & bulky like the ulna.
But now they're little beaks, and you're gone,
making my body a cage for their hunger – ah,
tonight's a long one.

Beau Hopkins was born in 1982 and grew up in rural Oxfordshire. He received his BA in French and Spanish from Oxford University. He then completed a graduate diploma in law at City University, London, and worked as an advocate in commercial debt. In 2009 he won the BAFTA/ Script Factory Serious Screenwriting Award and his screenplay is currently in development. He lives in London with his partner and daughter.

Edwin Kelly

Child Psychologist
From *Stones*
From *Birdsong Sonograms*
Coolisheal Pines

Child Psychologist

The boy placed his glass of water on the centre of my desk,
touched the thin meniscus and said
                        It feels like this
then pushed his finger through the water's skin.
I noted the refraction, his finger enlarged and broken.

In retirement I remember this, and dream of flies
hatching from flakes of my skin.
                        When I look in my mirror I see
beads of sweat. A moth, wings folded, on my shaving light.

by Edwin Kelly

from Stones

In times of widespread dissolution
(such as now, as always) when days are spent
suspended between double glaze,
caught in the blaze of an afternoon sun,

or caught in anxiety's especial fragrance
that your mind thinks only it can sense,
a molecular knowledge is being made known
so you no longer know when touching stone

whether or not the stone touched you; in
times like these, when rain itself seems
a solidness of grief you dare not walk in
and the concrete it beats is a crying reply,

the mind, meaning you, seeks an anchor,
finds no sense fit to furnish it one
so retreats within itself to seek
the stone-simple centre of being here.

from Birdsong Sonograms

The pipit's song:
        shark's tooth
                dangling
      on a string

The magpie's ratcheting:
        dust-storm
                diminishing
      the Roman forum

The goldcrest's chirp:
        guillotine
                in a hall
      of mirrors

The jackdaw's croak:
        fish-hooks
                dropped
      in clear ice water

The starling's whistle:
        wheat field
                scythed
      finally gathered

by Edwin Kelly

Coolisheal Pines

The entrance is through an old Cortina,
more rust now than metal, both dog-bed
and gateway through the overgrown briars
let wild to keep cattle out of the copse.
Seats ripped out and replaced with straw,
a scattering of bones, smell of damp dog,
cardboard and rot (this all happens before
I am born) with the vulnerable mongrel
bitch laid out where the back seat should be,
her teats clamped on by bundles of half-life
who whimper for milk even while drinking.
I push past, exit through the driver's door
and into the woods. In underwater light
the trees take on a calm terror and creak
without wind. I walk across a carpet
of pine needles, years old, take sponged steps
towards a small stream and see Nanan
scrubbing clothes against a rock, the foam
dissolving downstream. I call. No answer.
(This is before my mother is born.)
She hums a song with her back to me,
shoulders unhunched in their work.
I turn to the half-knocked cottage in the trees,
the back wall, hearth and chimney breast
still standing, and a mantelpiece covered
with unfilled picture frames. Tom sits
in his high-backed chair by the fire
poking at the hearth buried in pine needles,
their low smoulder more smoke than flame.
I sit with him, am ready to speak
about the things I remember, cornflakes
drenched in cow-warm milk, the gummy bite

Assorted Poetry

of calves in the shed, the carriage clock,
when the dog skulks back through the woods,
ears low to her head. Tom clicks his tongue
and she lies at his feet. His eyes are hidden
by his glasses, I cannot tell if he sees I'm here.
He lowers his hand to the dog's head.
She laps at milk from a small copper pan.

Edwin Kelly is from Garryarthur, Co Limerick. He also studied creative writing at University College Dublin. He has worked as a primary school teacher for a number of years and has organised writing workshops for children and adults. He is one of the founding members of the Quantum Sofa Poetry Sessions.

by Edwin Kelly

Timur Moon

Yellow Field
Cigarette Breaks
Rat Run

Yellow Field

We hung a gap in the woods and scaled a gate,
hemmed in by walls of hawthorn, corridors
of bramble; clambered, thorn-caught, nettle-stung,

through hedgerow; found ourselves in the beyond field
full of yellow, stretching far and wide
as the eye could take in, empty of all

but sun and sky, horizon and that crazy
sloping grass, bleached the colour of barley,
pale ochre, raw calico,

bright almost as lemons, and you slipped
your hand into mine and we ploughed on into Elysium –
hayfever field of GM crops, playground

for munchkins – corn and maize rolling over
into rapeseed, hay bales, and the sun
blazing chromium, like heaven, Wonderland,

some realm out of Disney or *The Wizard of Oz*.
You put a blanket out, we broke baguette,
cut tomatoes rough-hewn with your penknife,

buttered our bread, brought out gorgonzola,
and I partook of plastic ham, peeled
from a packet in slices of Day-Glo pink,

and as you're vegetarian, I did that alone;
and then we ate strawberries and clotted cream
and sure, there was wine, I liberated

by Timur Moon

from the bottle between my legs. And the result
splashed red on my lap, across my front, and you laughed
and flexed your legs, stretched out, went on absorbing

lunch and the sun, and we lay there, eyelids broiling
in an inner life of blindness, and the motes
behind my eyes swivelled with sunspots, beaming

lasers traced through the cosmos, travelling.
And I could gauge the curve of the earth turn, feel
hard ground beneath me, see the sky swirl – clouds

were moving as I watched them, but really you
were who I was watching, what you didn't know
was I had no way of helping it; my eyes

swam with the way you whelmed, and drank you in,
seen through the bloom, and blossom spattered my visuals
like bunting or something; maybe you felt them burning

into your back, because you leaned over, then you put
it on me, irresistibly – scandalised me
with a look; reached out, and in the mad

hour, drew me in, and if it wasn't
for the sun shrilling its white noise and the sky
screaming blue murder, I might have known

what you were thinking; or I would have told you
what I was, or tried to. So here goes.

Cigarette Breaks

i/
Nice when the sun's out, though,
said one man, sweeping leaves in a gale,
to another
who was trying to light a cigarette.

ii/
There'll be three along next,
said a man, long single, to the next, who had no job,
as they waited at a bus stop in the rain.
They both lit up to hurry the arrivals.

iii/
Go on then, pass us one, pal,
said the father-to-be to his friend, chugging away
after the meal was done.
Just don't tell you-know-who.

iv/
After every early morning's
detonating alarm, then coffee,
I light up, momentarily overtaken
by the faint lightheadedness of the blood rush.

v/
Feeling frowsy, mussed-up, she reached over
to the bedside table for her Marlboro Lights,
sparked up and felt the slow roasting of her lungs.
Save me a drag, will you, said the body beside her.

by Timur Moon

vi/
With a creaking throat, and the clock timing out,
he ground the fuming stub into the pavement,
descending the escalator
to join the stampede.

vii/
She tore the envelope open – hands trembling –
barely able to decipher
the good or bad news swimming in her eyes
as she cast about for a fag.

viii/
He swept through arrivals, cleared customs,
hauled his luggage and all
from the carousel, like a wanted man, jittery,
then putting the queues behind him, blazed up a burn.

ix/
On a stool in a foyer, alone,
turning the liquor round in his glass
under halcyon lamps, he gave in;
asked the barman for twenty B&H.

x/
At the foot of the plate glass tower, with the temps
and corpulent, heart-attack, bacon-sarnie bosses,
she stood in the nauseous gust
in a sea of butts, by the whirring waste disposal.

xi/
Discharged from the station after an all-night
grilling under striplights, unslept, wired
on adrenaline, he lit up, drew in deep
the dawn on the streets, and walked.

xii/
With music moving the walls
and the mad cacophony of crosstalk
rising to a crescendo each time the doors opened,
he stood on the doorstep shivering and gasping.

xiii/
When the heave and haul of writing came to a rest
he put a stop to the end of the line. Then he lit
a smouldering stick, took a long last lug,
and stubbed it out.

xiv/
Her lover obliging with a gilded flame
and languor dwelling in her doe eyes
and the lipstick on the tip a peachy blur,
the curling wisps of blue went up in smoke.

xv/
When I'd written it all up, and made the deadline,
clattering at the keys, and done a cut,
I slapped on a headline
and went for a smoke.

by Timur Moon

Rat Run

They buzzed the door, dressed head-to-toe in black,
from baseball caps and bomber jackets down
to their bovver boots; hustled in like bailiffs
or bouncers or some kind of hitmen, bristled and whiskered,
black-gloved hands bearing black briefcases,
stealing beady looks around the room;
a swivel-eyed and snout-nosed double act.
One of them did the talking, one was silent.

I explained about the massacred bananas,
savaged in their skins on the kitchen table,
and how I thought it must have been my flatmate
tripping home from a spree that must have involved
the bananas taking an almighty beating.
And seeing those bananas murdered in the morning,
he'd thought the same of me. That's when we knew
there were some hungry monsters in the kitchen.

So the men inhabit the kitchen, nostrils flaring,
drag out the dishwasher and ferret around
on all fours, crawl along the boarding,
assess the demolition site behind:
half the wall was torn up from the floor
so you could see the pipes behind the shredded plaster;
on a pile of rubble behind the pre-fab units
lay a mound of ravaged apple cores and nutshells.

So then I told them of my flatmate's apples
plucked from a bowl on the desk and, one by one,
rolled along the corridor and left
like the scene of a lynching, or summary execution
after the firing squad had done its work:
the butchered fruit, at two-foot intervals

Assorted Poetry

lined up like sacrificial offerings
in a ghoulish geometry of rotting heads.

And I told them of the thudding, no, the thumping,
that heavy mass of movement you could hear
come from behind the cupboards after dark;
The brazen way the vermin went out bingeing
and overran the kitchen every night;
how the contents of the dustbin got churned up
and thrown around in a nightly free-for-all;
and the sound of claws on corrugated roof.

*Back in Calcutta, Ajit would prise open
the manhole and go wading in the drains
through putrid standing swill, impaling rats
on his spear, like shooting fish in a barrel.
And suddenly a hairy, writhing creature's
dangling under my nose, skewered on a stick,
and I jump half out of my wits, and then see Ajit
beaming ecstatically from ear to ear.*

Here in the kitchen, the men describe the foxes
they'd stalked that morning halfway to the heavens
300 metres up, to the pinnacle
of the Shard, that latest plate glass skyscraper
rising vertically from the rubble,
reaching an impossible perspective
seventy storeys up, amid the overcast
and swirling skies, half a mile above.

They'd been living on the 67th floor
of Europe's highest building, in the clouds,
surviving on scraps the workers left. – You could abseil
into thin air, in one fell swoop
out of the blue around you, the quiet one said.

by Timur Moon

The city was a circuit board; its grid
lit up with diodes in the night, then dawn
was spread like a map in pink and grey beneath you.

And, just hearing him tell it, you're transported –
stomach stolen by vertigo at the prospect –
surveying the terrain through animal's eyes
looking out on the sprawl that only this morning
the foxes contemplated in the sky:
rabbit warren, rat run, anthill, molehill …
You could just slide out of the atmosphere, he said
with a distant look, go sailing down the river.

Timur Moon has worked as a reporter, feature writer, subeditor and gossip columnist for newspapers including the *Evening Standard, The Observer, The Times and The Express*. After graduating from Oxford, he worked in India and Pakistan, reporting for Al Jazeera, and later became art critic for *The National* in Abu Dhabi. He lives in London.
timurmoon@hotmail.com

by Timur Moon

Christopher Ogden

Mos Eisley Sestina
Waiting for Robbo
Pioneers
Manic Pixie Dream Girl
The Lookout View

Mos Eisley Sestina

You will never find a more wretched hive of scum and villainy ...
— Obi-Wan Kenobi, *Episode IV*

Episode IV: A New Hope
That first John Williams flourish gives *Star Wars* the force
of nature: *da-dah-dadada-DAAAA-dah!* God, George, no
one of us could forget that ocean of wrecked lights, two
Tatooine suns, the Death Star run, how Han outshot
Greedo! Still we're the drunks in the Mos Eisley bar,
each spectacle our liquor, hip idol, firebrand of mind.

Episode V: The Empire Strikes Back
Which film's cooler than *Empire*, that most dazzling of mind
tricks? Only *you* could muster little Yoda's X-Wing force,
AT-ATs staggering over snow as if leaving a Tyneside bar!
It's the warm guts inside a tauntaun, an inviting Pernod
drifting us through the clouds towards that windy Vader shot ...
That's impossible! Luke said. Repeat *this?* But you had to.

Episode VI: Return of the Jedi
So you did. And *Jedi* very nearly filled the sarlacc too,
a faultless three course meal. Oh, George, never *mind*
the Ewoks, but you gave the forest your best shot:
a lush and refreshing mojito! The Emperor's Force
lightning is suspect, and the ending's sentimental. No
matter: side effects of the 80s. You still raised the bar.

Episode I: The Phantom Menace
But how can we measure the wack sadness of Jar Jar,
commodity flap-clown, outcast designed to appeal to
six year olds? We understand why you couldn't say no,
George (after all, there's a new generation to be mined
with pod racers, slick CGI); still, *cruel* to turn the Force
into a cold science that fizzes in kids like an alcopop shot.

by Christopher Ogden

Episode II: Attack of the Clones
Here's where it starts to fall flat like a night out in Aldershot,
cellar-kept cask beer, *God Save The Queen* after a single bar ...
Politics *can* be action if you want it; you don't have to force
Yoda to do backflips or surprise rocket boosters inside R2.
The dialogue for Anakin ... What went through your mind?
You might as well have dressed a block of wood in chinos.

Episode III: Revenge of the Sith
But that's *nothing* to making the new Vader cry NOOOOO!
right at the end, a stinging tequila slammer, memories shot
to bits before that ... This man crushes throats, *with his mind,*
and you made him cry: the series' main villain utterly FUBAR!
So what if the rest of it's OK? No, this has to stop: you're too
far gone, getting lost to the perilous dark side of the Force ...

You're a wino, George. All this grandeur's addling your mind.
We own this establishment now. Sorry, we have to get shot
of you: you're barred. Leave, *please;* we don't want to use force ...

Waiting for Robbo
for Rob Brown

You think that you find yourself here out of politeness,
waiting for a friend at a riverside pub table, no guess
as to when he'll arrive. Nursing your pint of Guinness,
the man next to you (ex-serviceman, trousers pressed,
with a moustache, cigar-thick, that screams fustiness)
wants to start a conversation. Hesitantly, you express
your agreement, then realise too late; he's *obsessed*
with deadlock battles: the Pig War, Cold War, chess.

You try to gaze away into the river's evening laziness
to break things off, but then someone starts to press
the first few piano keys of Rachmaninov's *Elegie Es-moll* on one of the moored boats. The song depresses
you unusually. Then, in your moment of weakness,
he suggests another pint before you go. You say *Yes*.

by Christopher Ogden

Pioneers

The high school football team were called the Pioneers, and on their mural beside the bleachers we saw it again: that nebulous word, spirit. Wandering this suburb, we wondered if we'd missed it; the streets were spookily quiet, pristine, almost an abandoned set for a movie, lined with swanky boutiques, baskets full of flowers a bright Hollywood cerise. Sat in the ice-cream parlour with soda floats, we sat and thought of the students' gross-out jokes: all this was the basis for *American Pie*, a smash comedy that felt empty, adolescent, too wide. Later, at the lake by the school, we watched families with boats over evening barbecues, the water stretching out before us in widescreen, with a few Pioneers, swashbucklers in blue, hoisting a flag to a mast, sailing.

Manic Pixie Dream Girl

Three of us in the café saw the girl in the blue coat
with the St. Pauli bag, black, skull-and-crossboned,
as if she'd spent the last night tearing her throat
to punk rock in an underground dive. Barcelona
was full of girls like her. We wandered amazed
by the culture, only there to watch the football,
saying if only we'd been born some other place,
spoke the same language, or had the courage
to get past that mere idea before we walked away.

The Lookout View
Westward Ho!, for Talitha Black

In search of solace, I visited you, and we climbed up to the lookout
fixed from ruin, World War II. The Atlantic shimmered mystery
as sepia and youth blended around us: on the walls, a bright new
children's mural where starfish waved and seagulls flew, and out
the rocky cliffs, black ocean scars, wrecks maybe lived through.
Then I sensed an opening, some belonging twisting in the blue.

....

Christopher Ogden was born in Salford in 1989 and graduated from UEA's English Literature with Creative Writing BA with First Class Honours in 2010. At the time of writing he is planning his Masters dissertation, provisionally titled *Saturday At Three*, a collection of poems surrounding a single fictional football match.

by Christopher Ogden

Amy Ramsay

Grandfather Clock
Moldova
Fabergé
Elizabeth
Lies come slow
The Mother
David Dawes the Baker

Grandfather Clock

You left us the clock
with the fat chime
punctiliously wound –
a way of getting heard
each quarter hour.

Moldova

Name me the capital of Moldova
but he can barely look
talks of honeycomb instead –
says pulling honey is like extracting teeth
a dentist covering his mouth
administering a smoky anaesthetic.

I close my eyes, lap burnt heather
warm hands in gloves
burlap, hessian and pine
chewing the gum.

Dad's bees, a plethora of limbs
crystallised in combs, entombed –
a throbbing amberline liquid
fixing veins in petal wings.

Bring me quick an empty jar
an empty jar, no honey pot
and hum again as is the rhyme
he loves me, he loves me not.

by Amy Ramsay

Fabergé

He took them while they slept –
still warm, unhatched,
keeping on his tips (his luck)
a great count.

Rushing, she nearly stepped
on six;
perfectly wrapped –
still warm, unhatched.

Elizabeth

Her first son's death, she tasted in the well;
he'd played a private game on mossy brink.

Her second, born soft, flicked on flicked off
a third came slowly *E l i z a b e t h,*

Elizabeth on knees,
Elizabeth on shoulders.

Plump bright and chatter
so corners were filled

and fine bee stings,
nettles, these made her cry

but mostly she smiled
and drew pictures on glass
her fingers a squeak.

Or plaiting corn, laid on the floor,
peering at threads,
speaking under a breath
in a man's voice or a woman's.

by Amy Ramsay

Lies come slow

Lies come slow to me today, unsettled by before,
how everything was sharply focused, each needle point exposed,
the way the sun weighed on branches, dropping low enough

for dirt on hands, remembering dirt on hands
from when I was a child, the smell of worm-rich soil and
your hands yesterday, how they seemed to ask a question.

I saw some girls I knew today and lies came slow so
unseen birds sing up.

The Mother

He found me by the stack;
licked clean, still wet.

The seasons suited me –
fat hands, spit and pink in the right places.

In time he said: *If I don't take her I shall die!*
And then he went to fight.

A whelp's heart is much like a human's and so
they took that instead; built me a hut where

I bore Silvester, a great hunter,
raised on the milk of she-bear and wild sow.

First it was rabbits, clawing and screaming
banging heads, held tight by their soft ankles.

Hedgehogs amused him, plucked and cut;
barely audible.

Our horse – barely strong enough to walk
I put my foot down.

In time he said: *I've heard there's a dragon not far from here, you'll be my bait.*

I preferred the company of dragons;
traced each scale with whispering tips.

by Amy Ramsay

David Dawes the Baker

In my bed it turned me
sick, yeast rising
through floorboards.

Then there were pies,
pastries, cakes and bread.
I stood happily to these!

Bad dreams bring me
to the oven and in the calm
morning, I learn

of your sister (who died)
and your mother, who
didn't like your bread.

As the currants fall, you
share the secrets of teacakes,
how best to fold.

Teach me firmness,
the balance of hands –
economy of all but lard
and kindness.

Amy Ramsay was born in the Midlands and studied English at the University of Leeds. She is Editorial Assistant at *Stand* magazine and her work has featured in *Poetry & Audience*. She is currently living and working in Leeds, commuting to Norwich to complete her Masters.

by Amy Ramsay

Angus Sinclair

The Traditional Formal Logic
Self-Portrait in Antique Shop Window
Close

The Traditional Formal Logic
assembled from the text of the same name by W. Angus Sinclair

    Chapter I
    Propositions

These books are books whose leaves have not been cut.
The subject is *Boys*, man from his birth, his wishes
and ejaculations and so forth. Several involved with one another

or incompetently mismanaged, reading in other
orders. *Boys* are not interested in games but grammar,
the living organism, our own estranged tongue.

We have now reached the stage of seeing
not virtue but persons. Mortal as mortal being,
hard stones or diamonds or very hard things.

Chapter II
Symbols and Distribution

I should explain. That blue tits
are lovely little creatures
is such remarkable simplification.
I might take the inquirer out of doors
for the long songs of round vowels,
and entirely confine ourselves to forms
as forms. I no longer deal with how simple
it really is. A bluish tint on the wing,

is on the one hand a consequence
of necessary use of a given subject,
a symbol between four and five inches
of the class of birds. On the other hand,
when I am asked, I deny their olive-green
backs. Saying something like the following:

that bird emerging upside down
on the top branch, blue and white
and so forth, is without
regard to specific meaning.

Chapter III
Immediate Inference

Some poets are surprised to discover they exist at all,
some rectangles with equal and adjacent sides are squares.

This easily remembered form is between truth and validity,
somewhat casual and even loose in everyday thinking.

Chapter IV
Mediate Inference

And if we convert *A*
we get *I* – I am talking
of my early experiences.

> *This man, concluded or inferred,*
> *is the murderer.*

They haven't got tickets
and depend for their persuasiveness
on the existence of sensations.

> *Near the scene of the crime,*
> *he is building complex arguments*

From these two taken together
one derives a perfect figure,
playing its part in contradictory laws.

> *and prevents us from deducing*
> *the undistributed middle.*

Self-Portrait In Antique Shop Window
after Vivian Maier

You say, there's *nothing new under the sun*.
The words snap, decisive, as your shutter
records the confidence of fedoras,
spare time on the steps of the tenements,
gaggles of boys in apple-caps grappling.
All of them held inside your Rolleiflex.

Now forever at the newspaper stand
it's March 19th, bright Saturday morning
puddles through mirrors and windows, as though
we could see light as light. Today you find
yourself; half-presence reflected between
the glass panes of a shop-front. Eyes tipped up

and fixed outside the scene on the still point
you sought beyond the confines of the frame.

by Angus Sinclair

Close

Is this garden a south-facing garden?
I don't remember which star denotes north.
These TV antennas are weather vanes
for the modern age! you shout from the roof.

The Plough is a constellation of grease
turning on the surface of my coffee.
Our house is like other houses. Sometimes
at night I see unfamiliar cars,

they turn into our close, loop back around.
I am glad to see these small adjustments,
the turn in the road under swollen stars.
Pleased when storms interrupt our reception.

A hole in the bowl will leak on Leo,
you shout. The sky clears.

Angus Sinclair previously studied at Norwich University College of the Arts, where he first became interested in discrepancies between written and visual languages. His pamphlet *Another Use of Canvas* documents his small-time experiences as a professional wrestler in Norfolk.

by Angus Sinclair

Matthew Spence

Assen
Kitchen
Atlas
Lathkill
Trent
LISTEN

Assen

When the rain finished we took a bus into town,
stumbled through the flat greys and pinks
picked a bench to eat pizza by a deer park.

Everything was fresh and clean. The gulped air cooled
like cobbles, ravenous pigeons flapped in invisible slips
of wind

and I looked at you for a moment,
the stretch of all Europe in   your face
                                on every blade of grass:
droplets.

Kitchen

I'm in the kitchen making food   you're out walking in the green hills
collecting stones   spitting in the river
and the whole world is right here
     look at the dog-eared calendar   when the wind blows the dates shuffle
when a cat jumps on the window sill   you make me jump

by Matthew Spence

Atlas

early still-dark houses in jutted dawn
early horses with fog breath on the small hold
early office with cubist shadow lawn
early again-born Buddha disguised as a rock
early rock, perfect in blue field
early ducks testing the pond
early train rattling on forever-through-the-broad tracks
early smile pinned to a fence, Smack! you're
a kind of billboard
early medieval church sucked into the land
early unplanned children, idyllic in the lane
early lake of light, purple in the still-night dark, then
early spark of first sun, or is it truck lights?
early helicopter in the womb sky
early wood stream, sticks, car tyres
early lunch, memories, early entire town, the smell of toast,
ten years, two-stroke
early grazing cattle
early jumbling downstairs to the kitchen
as they were off to work
early as ever, and running to the window
and watching the old red car disappear

Lathkill

Fish. Dead on the bank, where the river's bend
curves like a hand
and you left me faster than the sky.

They have us
to thank

for this
un/fortunate state

in which our
height in space
is fate

and where
an *I*
is not an I-am-waiting-for-you-and-the-ferry-is-strange-on-the-steaming-water *I*,
but rather, rocky and moss-drenched in a park, by a still
green pool.

by Matthew Spence

Trent

down to the washlands
where the library is mess of glass,
where the last of the kids leave the playground.
Breweries beam their smog, distant hills are charcoal,
I sit on a bench and the ground is fat with water.

down to the washlands after college with Jess,
A horizon of flooded fields.
The low sun's reflection forms a golden sea.
She taps a joint in the silence
and the smoke joins the breeze.

down to the washlands while engines shunt carriages
and did you know this was *60 miles from the coast?*
Battered willows lull at the stream
a seamless expanse. A squirrel drags some paper
tangled in a branch.

down to the washlands to stare at my legs,
the talk of little birds wading in the shallows.
Trucks climb the hill, a barge churns water,
it's summer but the sun rises so late
I hardly know my own reflection.

LISTEN

in the town   by the wood
a grey disc sun
orange dusk rays like fingers
along your screen
shimmering beams of
headlamp-like-
light mist   if you like
that kind of thing
you'll love this   also
you were
saying something until
I inter-
rupted you
in the town   by the wood
you can get out of bed
just to stare at birds
hungry from sleep
should you like to eat something
the trees are full of food
reaching up to white clouds
take your pick
what you like pay
later   but
you were saying
something
in the town   by the wood
fields of live-
stock – take your pick
your own
we'll even let you
catch it kill it
eat it outdoors

by Matthew Spence

like a real natural cowboy!
in the town   by the wood
wind turbines cut the air
on TURBINE HILL
the smell of grass-smoke
gas   traffic-choked lanes
a real party
over-run with junk
half-sunk drinks
eternally the last ten minutes
(What's beyond the yard?)
in the town   by the wood
our angel the south-west is coming
and the castle is surrounded
by glinting cars
forget your day jobs
and come see the museum's
collection of war videos!
in the town   by the wood
glistening puddles where the roof
came off
holes in the road
a damp through-the-fog glow
rows of shops
shaved models
cheap shovels
trucks
perfectly shaped
vegetables
deals on coffins
deals on trains
tracking down lost friends
and
as I was saying
ladies and gentleman

sir
this whole load of things
your dreams
your no-longer-need-to-worry key
to peace
to a good night's sleep
freedom of speech
freedom of movement
government preserved beeches
with no nudity
at a special deal-rate
only from me
only today
only to you
you're/it's
all completely free

Matthew Spence is 23 and lives all over the place; currently he is in the East Midlands. His writing is influenced by the idea of 'stillness within movement'. He hopes to create a new kind of Zen Buddhist poetry.

by Matthew Spence

Eleanor Stewart

The Dead Sea
Apollo 14
Acorns
The Return of the Hunters
The Peasant Wedding Banquet
By The Icarian Sea

The Dead Sea

I knew he'd wished for years to study the mesas
in Jordan's Wadi Rum, but when the opportunity arose,
what to do with me, his wife? Could I travel in my fragile state?
Angelic with their white coats backlit by the lamps,
the three doctors nodded their assent: why yes, there were no
physical impediments to travel at this stage – so long as Madam
took care not to walk out in the midday sun, all would be well;
they'd heard the dwellings in the banded rocks of Petra
were superb, the Dead Sea, curious, too – though its precise
mineral properties were not yet known, Mrs Green,
wife of the eminent thalassotherapist, claimed that
after three weeks' bathing, all her ills were cured!
Indeed – this whispered with a furtive glance at me –
she gave birth to a son after just six months back at home.
Perhaps, if she did test the waters, Madam might be so kind
as to bring a sample of the salts on her return?
Yes, all in all there could be no harm to the proposed trip;
the change of scene would do her good,
it was high time for Madam to look forward now, not back.

So it was settled, the trunks and boxes packed,
the house shut up. We travelled east and by the spring
I was installed in lodgings in the care of Mrs Briggs,
a widow who, at sixty, put her fine complexion down
to a strict regime of Dead Sea mud baths twice a week.
She had five sons, and talked of nothing but her grandchildren;
producing christening ribbons, snips of hair and milk teeth
and lamenting that she'd never once set eyes on them, though
the eldest boy was due to sail from England just next year.
In all her volubility she didn't heed my silence,
nor my regular retreat back up the stairs to the quiet clasp
of shuttered windows and a canopied bed.

by Eleanor Stewart

I wondered how much my husband had told her of our troubles.
He'd left for Petra with a string of laden donkeys and a guide,
with strict commands that I should bathe each day.
I longed to get away from Mrs Briggs's incessant prattle.
Draped head to toe in white against the sun, with a servant girl in tow,
I went down to the shore one morning,
early on, when the water was still swathed in mist.

The rocks grew jagged, dredged in glittering salt, the closer
to the sea that they advanced. The water glistened with an oily sheen
and was strangely heavy to the touch, setting my skin tingling
like a mild electric shock. I'd been warned not to let it splash
into my eyes or mouth – the stinging was apparently acute.
I floated on my back without a sound; trying to discern
the ridge of mountains on the farthest shore. A year ago
they'd have been hidden behind my own growing mound.
How long we waited! Seven years of monthly disappointment.
When he arrived stillborn, my husband wept, cradling him
to his chest – a miniature in palest lapis lazuli – starved of oxygen
the doctors said. I did not weep, could not begin to speak
my anguish – it was enough to suffer it. After six months
my husband urged me to stop dwelling on the past, the doctors,
too, said there was no use in looking back. Was that not the crime
of Lot's wife? She was standing somewhere in those distant hills,
and here I was – no waves to break my thoughts – confined
within this barren saline sea; mute as a pillar of salt,
defined by my own concentrated, crystallising grief.

A sudden movement caught my eye – the only sign of life
in such harsh and hostile waters. A crane fly, trapped;
wings flickering desperately in an attempt to fly and escape
the cloying water. It would have a long and drawn out death,
struggling for hours against the salt and sun.
It was too late to save it, but I spared it that, at least,
and pressed its flailing form into the sea.

I thought of drowning, too. Would the salt preserve my corpse?
I imagined my husband coming back to find his wife
laid out – an unyielding slab of flesh – embalmed.
Accidents did happen. Mrs Briggs had said at least one
poor soul drowned each year; people did not expect to float
so tried to swim then swallowed brackish water; panicked; choked.
But the sea itself resisted me, as if it somehow knew
that brought so low as this, within Earth's lowest place,
my death would be no mishap. Each way I turned I seemed
to be denied; the buoyant water tipped me up
within a blink, unceremoniously flipped me on my back:
it was impossible to sink.

From far away I heard a distant shout – the maid –
I had drifted too far out. I made my way to shore,
feeling cautiously for land beneath my feet then, knee-deep in water
– Ah! – I slipped and split my skin upon a salt-encrusted rock.
The wound screamed with the pain and I screamed too,
the foulest words I knew, tears streaming down my cheeks;
the sun, the salt, the sky, my absent spouse, the fertile Mrs Briggs
and all her sons, the doctors back in Harley Street
– all suffered my abuse. My voice cracked – long unaccustomed
to such violent use. The last time I'd shouted had been
all those many months ago, in the final hours of labour.
I wiped my cheeks and rose a little wobbly to my feet.
The maid stood flabbergasted with my flannel gown in hand,
whilst nearby a gaggle of spectators looked on.
Who knows what they thought of me? Mad Englishwoman,
shouting curses at the sea. Surely a maniac?
But, on the contrary, I'd never felt so lucid. I declined
the servant's outstretched hand and hobbled
back up to the house, where, in my room, I flung
the shutters wide and sat out on the balcony,
to gaze at the scorching sun in its sky of lapis lazuli.

by Eleanor Stewart

Apollo 14

The seeds were stowed and carefully confined
– the canister not quite six inches square.
Fir, Redwood, Sweetgum, Sycamore and Pine
were hand-selected, chosen to go where
no seed had ever gone before. Encased
in metal, within a larger metal shell:
a capsule full of light and life that raced
out of the atmosphere, so that Earth fell
away and the seeds lost what little weight
they'd ever had. Yet as the shuttle wound
in orbit, they harboured thoughts to germinate,
to lay claim to the dust and rocks, but found,
once on the dark side of the moon, the clasp
of far-flung stars to be beyond their grasp.

Acorns

An oak tree in September:
nodules cluster at the tips of branches,
little green galaxies that might be acorns
in fœtal form, but in fact turn out to be galls,
privateered by the wasps.

Some acorns shy from life
and stay huddled purple in their cups,
while others are coaxed out by a false wind
and lay per se as bruises on the ground
– miscarried.

Certain ones are bolder,
straining from the shells that hold them until
– surely with a pop – they're free to fall
to earth, dip-dyed white, yellow
and life-affirming green.

The last of them endure;
a deep bronze and hoarded like coins
until their weight is burdensome.
Once dropped they scatter,
rolling downhill, seeking space.

by Eleanor Stewart

The Return of the Hunters
after Bruegel

The mountains, fields and roofs are dredged in white,
everywhere you look there's snow. The trees' stark
branches bristle at the cold, the sharp bite
of the wind has snatched their leaves as the dark
nights draw further in. Water's turned to slate –
ponds muted village greens on which two crows
strut by a bridge and specks of people skate.
Beside the inn, its sign all crooked, glows
a fire that's shivered itself to a blaze.
Two aproned figures stoke it high, engrossed
in the flames, no time to avert their gaze
to the hunters who've returned with their host
of dogs. The lightness of their loads belies
their homeward steps, heavy as the laden skies.

The Peasant Wedding Banquet
after Bruegel

The barn heaves with guests,
more piling in to fill the benches
round the white-clothed table.
They're decked out in their best:
jackets of crimson, duck-egg blue and green,
the women in their cleanest bonnets,
men in caps – one tasselled,
another used to stash a wooden spoon,
a boy's with a peacock feather, bobbing.
The door, superfluous against
the tide of well-wishers, is taken off
its hinges, carried on birch poles between
two sturdy men in great clodhopping shoes,
bearing bowls of porridge so thick
that even when the server accidentally
tips one it does not slop out.
The bride sits underneath her crown,
hair flowing loose, eyes lowered
in a contemplative smile,
her cheeks grown ruddy in the heat.
The groom is nowhere to be seen;
perhaps he's slipped out to take a piss
or simply to escape the bawdiness
of a pair of heaving bagpipes.
A basket heaps with empty jugs next to
the peacock-feathered child who sucks
traces of porridge from his thumb
(along with a quantity of dirt).
From underneath the table pokes a nose –
a dog – hopeful for scraps; his master
deep in conversation with the monk

by Eleanor Stewart

who patiently ignores
the thumping tail against his legs.
The barn swells with bagpipes, laughter, talk;
the scent of fresh cut birch
released by the rub of thighs on benches,
muddled with ale-soaked breath and sweat;
the warmth of straw bale walls. Later,
they will dance.

By The Icarian Sea

It was a good orange, firm
but with a spring to it.
Shepherd cast a glance
towards his sheep (all there)
then dug a fingernail in.
It was a good orange.
He proceeded, with care,
to carve out a land for himself,
smiling when the peel came away
in one piece in his hand.
He turned it this way and that
and pondered on what map it could be,
if he knew any geography.

He considered throwing it
at Ploughman, a little to his left,
but thought the better of it
(Ploughman had muscles).
Instead he threw it out to sea
in a high, wide arc,
where the wind caught it
and turned it to a scudding,
orange-bellied gull.

Shepherd watched its flight
leaning from the cliff-edge,
devouring juicy segments.
There was a mass of foaming
feathers amongst the crests
and peaks of waves and more
carried by the breeze.
One caught, sticky, in his fingers

by Eleanor Stewart

and he wondered what strange
bird it came from.

The orange peel fell.

And in his last breath
before the water,
Icarus thought that the
sun had decided
to fall with him.

Eleanor Stewart was born in 1989 and grew up in Scunthorpe. She completed a BA in English Literature and Creative Writing at UEA in 2011 and received the Malcolm Bradbury Prize for best undergraduate Creative Writing dissertation. She is the first recipient of the Ink Sweat & Tears Poetry Writing Scholarship.

by Eleanor Stewart

Cutter Streeby

Lizard
I died on a brilliant day like this:
The Act of Capes
~~Letter from a New City to an Old Friend~~
Wind Farm

Lizard

Take your hand and cup it.
Press your fingers and thumb together,

like when your ears were cold and you wanted warmth,
or when you still believed you could hear the ocean.

Close your eyes. Take your hand, rounded like a coracle or shell,
turn it over onto your child's abdomen, or the abdomen of your lover.

Cover the belly button. Close the edges down completely. Imagine
that world's horizons, its muffled darkness, the overtones of red;

imagine the burble of intestines, the warmth and moisture of flesh –
now a tornado-gray light, a single swirling drop

nosing its way down from the sky of your palm
to the plane of the umbilical scar, imagine the heat from your hand

taking root: the light, finding flesh, flares briefly through the capillaries.
Breathe in – the light pulls back from these red tributaries: a waterfall

lifting in reverse. Sieved by flesh, the light is silvery again,
and shivers against the cup of your hand like mercury.

Hold. The light gathers together, hangs from the roof of your palm,
trembles into
a lizard you dangle over a well: it scrabbles, arches itself backwards,

it claws and hooks upwards
biting against itself and that which holds it. Now the release:

by Cutter Streeby

a piece of your element coming unstitched. Imagine the creature's panic,
its chimera tail whipping once over the abdomen as it drops

down into the well,
          into the stomach –

imagine the sound it makes as it settles to the bottom.
Breathe out. Lift your hand

– say softly, 'You're mine,'
or, 'I love you.'

See how its reptile light
skitters under your loved one's skin? Remember how it fades
from white to
                blue to
                        orange
                                to flesh.

I died on a brilliant day like this:

thunderheads wrapped the mountain to the west of my house,
to the east, sky so clear I could map the gradation of blues
as they moved from horizon's royal to the sun's pearl shell.

Look at the design of this canopy,
you'd said once, in a forest outside of town.
Your head flung back, oblivious to the brambles around your thighs.
It's like the layout of a city.
See that oak there, in the middle?
A central monument ...

Searching from right to left,
your arm still half-up, forgotten
until you pointed to the copulas you'd needed to find,
And that blue jay policing her stoop,
those finches, jobless in the hackberry,
a spider web there, stalled-out under construction, that trail,
a highway of wildlife when we aren't here, and I bet, if we waited till nightfall,
that bole would hold our Grandfather Owl with his golden eyes
and flexing claws.

But I could never see it like that when we were both alive.
To me, death was a little figurine bobbing somewhere
in the backwater of our aquarium town
with its costume rocks and manicured lawns,
its neat rows of white headstones each with an unassuming name;
each from the other offset at precise angles – all together a perfect
field of marble.

I didn't understand the urgency you'd felt since birth. Why you'd
wanted to leave,
why you seemed inconstant even to yourself.
I think I could understand it now, after the call I got last December.

by Cutter Streeby

After my own death that winter in the desert.

I had assumed it was an affinity to death that let you live everyday as the last of your
          kind, chest out, full stride, burning to touch everything under the sky –

But now, like you, I've shed my conceptions of earth and its attendant concerns: winter, spring, summer, fall. Your quick breath and trapped eyes have snapped into my own canopy, one grown from the undergrowth into a delicate lace of leaves and light. I see most of those patterns now, so a breeze trembles the world up there.

I'm different since your death. Slower. Not less full of light, just more aware of its pieces. I can hear the worms shift the earth three meters below ground, and even the ocean plate sliding under my city raises a symphony now. Music on music veined with music.

Twenty years ago, I tunneled away from your funeral blind, translucent, recalling the smell of wet dirt one spring, and how you'd always whistle notes to a melody I'd never heard. But it's been a while, brother, and I've been learning what you always knew.

So this morning, with my legs hanging over the edge of this bed, I'm going to flex my feet. I'm going to stand up. I'm going to shave in my cracked mirror and pour a cup of coffee. I'm going to step off this back porch into autumn's light rain and look through burnished eyes over a field still gray in the dawn.

Today, I'm going to disappear without a note to anyone.
Today I'm gone, searching for this year's last red mandevilla.

The Act of Capes

Enter Luck,
grinning. Angular.
Cross down stage right–
cue
The Flying Dutchman.

Luck: *(opened-mouthed)*

(pause, listening)

(slapping at fly,
eyes and head
mimic flight path)

Enter Bat, bouncing from ceiling.
 (Obviously cardboard –
 Sequined wings of markered-black
 wax paper.)

Luck *(falling backwards, scrambles up)*

Bat dances on
fishing strings
revealing the marionette.

Luck Flees.

Exit stage left.

by Cutter Streeby

~~Letter from a New City to an Old Friend~~   [SEAside   Gra-
i.m. Ronny Burhop 1987-2010   ffiti]

[*adjust*   Even the white noise here is different –
   trACKing]   there's no boulevard, no blue ~~and breathing~~
               ocean. The streets – more quiet now, winding
               through ~~rain, hidden~~ parks and open markets –
                                        [*chriiiiiiing*]
               are cobbled, and twist off into alleys
               less sinister than ours. There's ~~history~~   [RE*prise*]
               ~~in the~~ street names, true – but ~~the mystery~~,
               the footsteps' muffled click, the concrete sea
bRZeE
               ~~rolling below my window~~ is tame,
               bloodless …
                          [BRiX '98]
               We fell off ~~the world~~ for years in LA.   [SoDen

               I can only remember the haze now,   eAcH   corP.
               ~~how our vista was never really clear~~   oWn
               of smog, or planes, or neon bellied clouds.   a *sOul?*]

               I split. Left you standing with a pocket
[*My* grambag   full of lock-
                 of   less keys, a few bucks, two lighters and I
     tRixY   drove ~~the forty miles~~ back home. Years later,
rEds]   I'm hoping, perhaps we can just look back,
tuchhhh –   – MID*A*Z
               recall it before the cards were flipped –
               ~~our own Cassidy and Sundance era?~~   (EPIX
                                                   x
               I turned my back on California,   *X*)
               on ~~those two-for-one, from out the Honda~~
[Ma*lverde*]   ~~hustlers, sunburned illegals~~, *los santos*…
               And I have thought about nothing else, since.

Assorted Poetry

[oUr buRnT –

I heard ~~about your dazzling surrender.~~
Guess I should ask ~~'from whose bourn' and all that~~,
but I can't fucking see how it matters.

oUt   SCAPE]

Anyways, it's probably December
right now in your coastal town, every crow   *JauREZ –*
crowding the power lines, jostling. Each one   *Bosnia*
vacant, thinking only of ~~its single~~   *del SUR**
~~green walnut~~, the distance to the pavement.

by Cutter Streeby

Wind Farm

here is my flag
        the size of a tank
whipping in the blue Viagra sky

here the billionaire's
        Bvlgari bangles   her Maybach
          and the green rows of trees
      standing at ease
as she goes winding down Mulholland Drive
        as she comes   in from some island
descending on Rodeo Drive

here the hit new series
        red-bowed and candied
conceived of freedom and glory   by God's own PR scheme

here's my people's one constant
          consolation
            our junkyard of stars
clattering around Chateau Marmont

here is Yankee Stadium
        Whitehouse Stadium
        Yale Harvard Stanford
      our articulate politicians
and Vegas of the Bristling Lights

here's the ocean of my nation
        with the waves of its greatness
treasuring its foreign shores

here are the beachcombers spin-doctors tabloid readers and the academics the single
>mothers single fathers and the failed sport-stars editors
>producers and the plastic needle manufacturers

and here, behind my eyes, idling in the cave of my skull,
>a Ferrari engine
>>that purrs and purrs and purrs

Cutter Streeby is a graduate of the University of California, Riverside. He holds an MA from King's College, London and has published poems and translations in many American journals. He lives with his wife and son between California and Bangkok, where he is studying Thai poetry. Contact: cutter.p.streeby@gmail.com

by Cutter Streeby

Hayden Westfield-Bell

Downturn
The Rationalist
Thirty-Six Hour Shift
The Falling Down
Portraits

Downturn

That day
the sun tore
at our eyes.

Now we bob;
heads hovering
over hands
in hope that
when that final
shuffle shears us
from our shoulders
we won't be

headless.

by Hayden Westfield-Bell

The Rationalist

Pleasing the ears,
but we can't say
enough to fill those sneaking
gaps between our worlds.

I'm sorry, I am.
I am, I'm sorry.

It was always that
– worms as words –
a gentle slither, drooling, dribble
of a matter turns so suddenly
to a downpour, the pond fills
and the frogs slip out
in a smooth oozing
of bellies, and the watermill
continues to churn
and churn.

I saw him earlier,
when he was bawling
and falling; tearing
about the floor
for spare bones.

But the words don't work:
fall about in
        clusterfucks
barely managing to keep line.

But they have to carry on.

Pick up the bags beneath
their eyes and throw them over
worn shoulders, for the long
walk home.

Thirty-Six Hour Shift

A somnambulant walk
of tired tights pulled
over smooth bores.

The pleats? In disarray,
far from the ironed yesterday.

by Hayden Westfield-Bell

The Falling Down

The knives and forks
are crossed on the plates
in the kitchen,

the pots and pans
we used last night swim
in a pool of cold water.

Two used cups sit
quietly on the coffee table
by the sofa.

It's mid-afternoon,
and the rain lashes
at the windows,

outside, the birch
tree swings wildly
in the wind.

The bedroom upstairs
is uneasily clean;
the drawers pushed-to.

Your washed
clothes are absent
from the bedside cabinet.

I look outside,
out over those other
houses and think of you,

wandering home
wrapped in plastic,
bags on your back

banging against
your hips in that vicious
falling-down.

by Hayden Westfield-Bell

Portraits

Sitting with shutter eyes,
thinking of all the left behind
children sleeping in the park,
biting their lips, wondering
what a warm house smells like.

The warm feeling slipping
between your thighs
makes you think of the soft
oozing of caramel from
your favourite chocolates.

He'd laugh later, perhaps
bending over and holding
his stomach whilst his mouth
opens-closes-opens-closes,
gaping for water.

Maybe she'll laugh too;
throwing herself over the
walls like that time she'd left
her heart behind in that noisy,
cramped tent last summer.

Hayden Westfield-Bell has a keen interest in postmodern and transgressive literature, as well as continental philosophy. His poetry is often informed by the themes of space, modernity, emotional/psychological displacement, and critical theory. His work has previously appeared in *Popshot: The Love Issue*.

by Hayden Westfield-Bell